D0131586

The Middle Ages

Castles, Kings and Knights in Shining Armor

by
Lorraine Conway

illustrated by Linda Akins

Cover by Janet Skiles

Copyright © Good Apple, Inc., 1987

ISBN No. 0-86653-400-8

Good Apple
A Division of Frank Schaffer Publications, Inc.
23740 Hawthorne Boulevard
Torrance, CA 90505-5927

Introduction

The period of history known as the Middle Ages lasted about one thousand years, from 500 A.D. to 1500 A.D. It began as the Dark Ages, the stormy period of time that marked the disintegration of the great Roman Empire. That same empire that once spread law, order and language to the civilized Western world by the fifth century could no longer defend, control and maintain the territories it had conquered in its golden past. The barbarians from the North picked and plundered their way across Great Britain and Europe with cunning savagery ending the classical period of Roman culture and beginning an age of turmoil. From this age of turmoil, the men and women of the Middle Ages, possessed with the great instincts of survival and justice, laid the foundations for the great Ages which were to follow. In this book you shall learn about the people who lived in the Middle Ages, their heroes, costumes, laws and many of the things that made the Middle Ages a unique period of time.

Time Line for the Middle Ages

The Middle Ages lasted for about one thousand years. Ten important events which took place during that period of time are listed below. Use the dates and information to fill in the time line provided for you on the next page. You may wish to add other dates and information as you study the Middle Ages.

520   St. Benedict established the first monastery at Monte Cassino, Italy. He drew up a set of rules for the monks, which included vows of obedience, poverty and manual labor.

800   Charlemagne was crowned ruler of the Holy Roman Empire. This act symbolized a union of the church and state.

1066   William invaded and conquered England. He defeated King Harold who was killed at the Battle of Hastings. William brought feudalism and culture from France to England.

1096   First Crusade began. The Crusades were armies of Christians from all over Europe who marched to the Holy Land to regain lands captured by the Turks. The First Crusaders took the city of Jerusalem but paid a very heavy price in lives.

1147   Second Crusade was launched. This Crusade is generally considered to have been a failure.

1189   Third Crusade was one of the more successful. In it King Richard the Lion-Hearted obtained certain privileges for Christians from the Turkish ruler, Saladin.

1202   Fourth Crusade launched. In this Crusade the original purpose of the Crusades was abandoned, and the Crusaders burned and sacked many cities and villages on their route. They never reached the Holy Land.

1215   King John of England was forced to sign the Magna Carta. The Magna Carta gave some basic rights to the people and also said that the king was not above the law.

1291   Fall of Acre marked the end of the Crusades. Acre, the last Christian city in the Near East, was lost to the Turks.

1348   The black plague swept England and Europe. It was estimated that one out of every five people in England died. Spread by rat fleas, the disease is characterized by the victim turning dark purple in his last hours of life due to respiratory failure, hence the name, black plague.

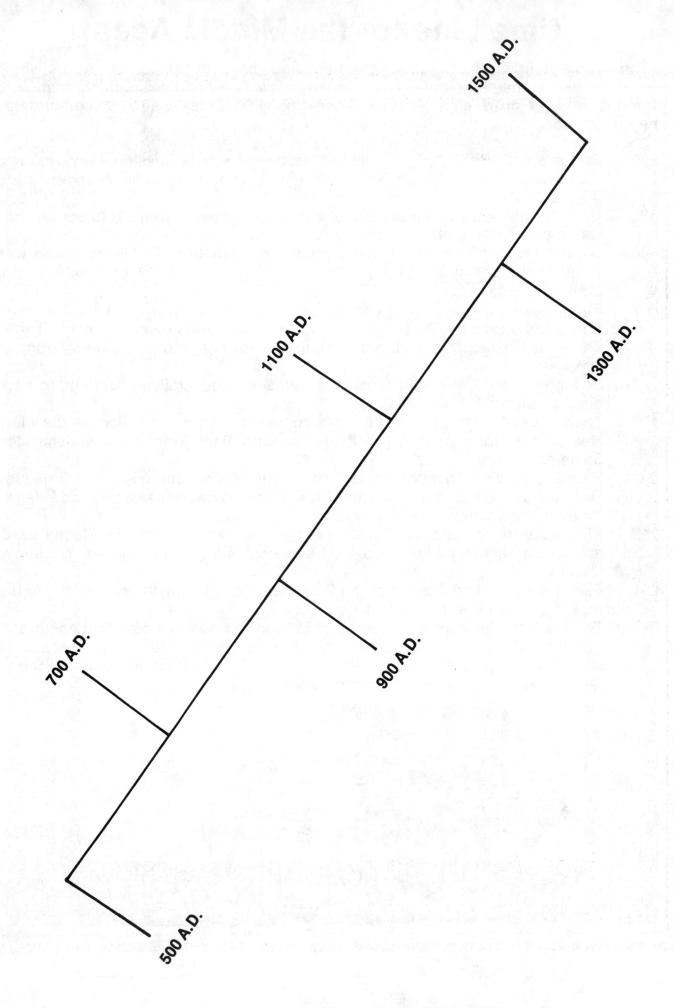

"What Saye Ye?"

English spoken in the Middle Ages was very different than it is today. Chances are if you were transported back in time to England in the Middle Ages, you would be unable to understand much of what was being said, as the spellings and pronunciations of many words were not the same as they are now. Some words that were common in the late Middle Ages were put into expressions below. Try to match the expressions on the right to their modern meanings on the left. A good dictionary will help you, if you need assistance.

_____ 1. She was pretty.

_____ 2. He didn't keep up with his contributions to the church.

_____ 3. She had a very nice cloth (scarf) covering her head and chin.

_____ 4. An excellent meal was prepared.

_____ 5. She was witty.

_____ 6. Come and have fun with us.

_____ 7. He is quite wealthy.

_____ 8. His horse had difficulty walking in the mud.

_____ 9. Cheer us up.

_____10. She was on a small horse.

_____11. Listen to me, sweetheart.

_____12. The priest had a big church and many parishioners.

a. "Good victuals were served."

b. "Come join our merry company."

c. "A comely lass was she."

d. "She was well-wimpled."

e. "A ready tongue was hers."

f. "His mare floundered in mire."

g. "Jolly us now."

h. "Wide was his parish."

i. "His tithes were in arrears."

j. "Pray hear me, true love."

k. "He had goods enough."

l. "She rode a palfrey brown."

Charlemagne

Charlemagne was a giant of a man in history and in stature. He stood six feet four inches tall, which was an unusually great height for a man of his time. He was also powerfully built with large shoulders and chest. His massive build was made more curious by the fact that he was the son of a ruler called Pepin the Short, King of the Franks. When Charlemagne succeeded his father, he extended his kingdom to include not only all of present-day France but much of Germany and parts of Italy, Bavaria and Spain. These lands became known as the Holy Roman Empire, and Charlemagne was crowned emperor.

Charlemagne was well-educated in both Latin and Greek and showed great interest in the preservation and spread of knowledge; he considered himself guardian of the Christian faith and spread Christianity to the many lands he conquered. At the same time he promoted education, art, commerce and farming. He also established a system of law and order.

After Charlemagne's death, his son, Louis the Pious, was unable to hold the empire together. Louis's three sons at the Treaty of Verdun in 843 A.D. further divided the kingdom into three parts, one part for each. This division gave rise to many wars between France and Germany which were to continue for centuries. With no strong central power to look to for protection, free men began to go to their local lords for aid, thus paving the way for the system called feudalism.

The top map on the next page shows Charlemagne's empire before it was divided. Color Charlemagne's empire with a color to suit you.

The bottom map shows how Charlemagne's empire was divided between his three grandsons at the Treaty of Verdun. Use three different colors to show each division. Compare these areas to a present-day political map of Europe. You will find one on page 4.

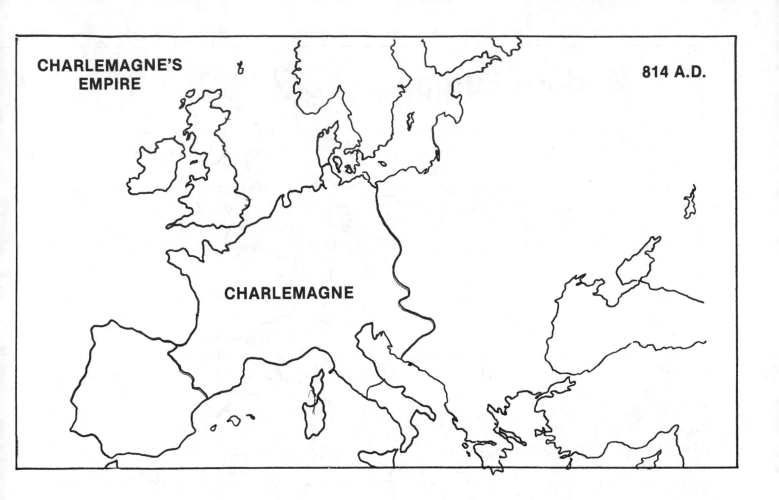

CHARLEMAGNE'S
EMPIRE

814 A.D.

CHARLEMAGNE

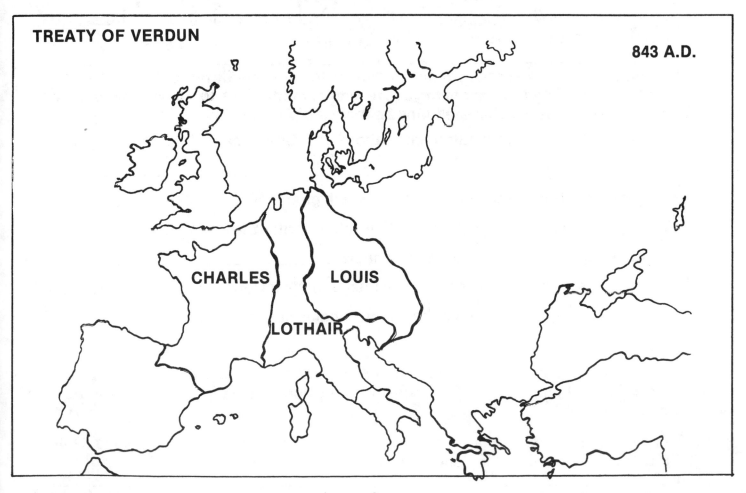

TREATY OF VERDUN

843 A.D.

CHARLES   LOUIS

LOTHAIR

Modern Europe

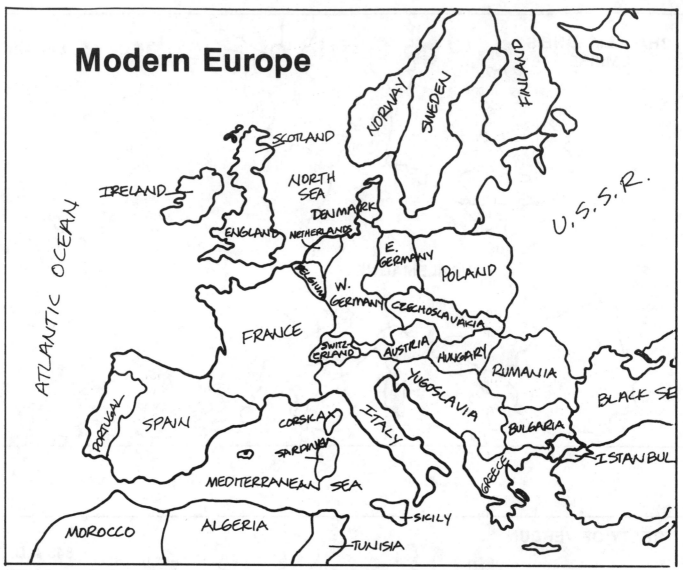

The boundaries of present-day European countries are very different from those during Charlemagne's reign. Compare the above map of modern Europe to the maps on the preceding page to answer the questions below.

1. What three great modern European nations did Charlemagne's Empire include?

   _____

2. Much of present-day France was given to which grandson? _____

3. Which grandson inherited most of Italy along with Switzerland and territories extending northward to the English Channel? _____

4. Which grandson inherited great parts of East and West Germany? _____

5. Did Charlemagne extend his empire far into what is now modern Spain? _____

6. Did Charlemagne conquer England? _____

7. Discuss how history might have been changed if Charlemagne's empire had not been divided. Include in your discussion the effects on language and culture of modern Europe.

8. Do you think there would have been fewer wars in Europe after Charlemagne's death if much of France, Germany and Italy had remained one great nation? Why or why not? _____

1066—The Battle of Hastings

The year 1066 is one of the most famous dates in history. It was in the spring of that year a French duke, William of Normandy, began his preparation for the conquest of England. Because William was a cousin of a former king of England and because he was married to an English noblewoman, Matilda of Flanders, he felt he had a just claim to the English throne. When September came, William felt his troops were ready. In crowded longboats filled with men, horses, and armor, the Normans crossed the channel and landed on the shores of England.

King Harold, leader of the English, had been alerted by his scouts weeks beforehand. He gathered his troops and took his position at the top of a hill, near a twisted apple tree. From there he commanded his men to build a defense of tree trunks and branches. From the top of the hill, he flew his standards, one a dragon and the other the gold embroidered figure of a fighting man. His army, which consisted of row after row of warriors armed with double-edged axes, settled themselves on the hillside.

William also had scouts, and they were eagerly waiting for him when he landed to inform him of Harold's position. Duke William rested his men several weeks until he was sure they were ready before advancing toward the English. Early on October 14th William ordered his troops forward. When the Norman troops were about a mile away in their march to do battle, they stopped to put on their coats of mail and make their final preparations. The Normans, who were used to fighting on horseback, called themselves chevaliers, from the French word *cheval*, meaning horse. The chevaliers were their main striking force composed of knights and other men called sergeants, who were soldiers on horseback. They also had foot soldiers armed with bows and arrows to protect the men on horseback. The English did not battle on horseback; their forces were composed mainly of foot soldiers armed with spears and axes.

The battle took place on October 14, 1066. William and his Norman knights charged bravely up the hill. King Harold's men struck back with heavy blows against them and their horses. Wielding their large double-edged axes, Harold's forces turned back the Norman attacks again and again. Casualties were so heavy it was written that the hill was slick from blood, but both sides fought on. Two of Harold's brothers were slain; still he ordered his men to hold their ground. Exhausted as they were, the Saxons found courage in their standards flying in the wind and their king urging them on. Leading his men, King Harold was suddenly struck in the face by an arrow. The wound put out his eye and he fell to the ground in pain. Shortly thereafter, the disheartened English began to break ranks and flee into the surrounding woods. The Normans soon broke through their lines and Harold was slain. The dragon and the fighting man were cut down. Without their leader, their standards, their hope, the rest of the Saxons ran for their lives. The Battle of Hastings was over; the Normans had won.

William was crowned King of England on Christmas Day in Westminster Abbey. He spent much of his remaining life crushing revolts against him and waging military campaigns. William the Conqueror, as he became known, died in 1087 at the age of fifty near Mantes, France. He died as he had spent much of his life, fighting, but unlike King Harold, not from the wound of an arrow or the blow of an ax; William was killed when his horse fell and crushed him.

1. After the Battle of Hastings the women of Bayeux (pronounced buy-you), France, embroidered a piece of linen cloth over two hundred feet long and about twenty inches wide. This tapestry gives us a detailed description of the battle, arms, costumes and manners of the Normans. The information for the tapestry was supplied by the returning Norman knights. Research the Bayeux tapestry and sketch a scene from it.

2. In 1066 the Battle of Hastings was a stunning victory for the French soldiers on horseback. In 1346 English soldiers proved that they could withstand the charge of chevaliers at the Battle of Crecy (pronounced Cray-see). Research the Battle of Crecy and contrast it to the Battle of Hastings. Tell about the new weapon introduced at Crecy and its effect on armor.

People of the Middle Ages

Write the names of the people of the Middle Ages on the blanks provided on the next page. When you have finished, answer the questions at the bottom of this page.

1. *Knights-Crusaders.* Noblemen who sought to help recapture the Holy Lands from the Turks were Knight-Crusaders. *Crusader* comes from the Latin word *crux,* meaning cross. Crusaders often used the cross as a symbol.

2. *Serfs.* The serfs owned nothing. They lived on the lord's land, grew their own food and worked for the lord of the manor in his fields. They had no freedom. When necessary they fought the lord's battles. For all this they received protection.

3. *Nuns.* Religious women who left their homes to live together in order to save their souls were called nuns. The church welcomed all and no doubt many women entered nunneries to escape poverty.

4. *Shepherds.* Tending the sheep of the manor was the job of the shepherds. It was lonely and often unrewarding work.

5. *Noblewomen.* The ladies of the castle supervised the upbringing of their children, gave instructions to their servants on the day-to-day running of the castle. They spent some time making medicines from herbs and tending to the poor. If they were able to read, they taught reading to the pages. In their spare time they sewed or worked on tapestries.

6. *Monks.* Men who left the company of ordinary men to live together away from worldly temptations and affairs were called monks. They took vows of obedience, poverty and chastity. Their first concern was to save their own souls. Many became well educated, and as time went on monasteries became centers of learning.

7. *Pilgrims.* Medieval Christians made pilgrimages to the Holy Land to visit the places where Jesus lived and died. The travelers who made their way to these lands were called pilgrims. They traveled great distances to receive special blessings and to ask forgiveness for their sins.

8. *Troubadours.* No one is certain when troubadours began to appear. We know that most of their songs dealt with love between knights and ladies, of gallant deeds the knights performed and the inspiration of their ladies for those deeds.

9. *Bishops.* The Bishops were noblemen of the church. They sometimes ruled over large land holdings and had knights under them. The Church stood for mercy, piety and dignity of all before God. For many of the poor, rising in the ranks of the church was their only chance to become the equal of a noble.

Questions:

1. Compare three of the depicted people of the Middle Ages to their modern-day types and tell how their roles have changed.
2. Describe how a modern nun might be dressed.
3. List by name some current and popular "troubadours." Compare their position in society and how they work to the troubadours of the Middle Ages.

People of the Middle Ages

A. _____

B. _____

C. _____

D. _____

E. _____

F. _____

G. _____

H. _____

I. _____

7

Lord Randal

Ballads, often sung and spread by troubadours, were to the ordinary people of the Middle Ages not only literature, but cherished entertainment as popular music is to us today. The ballads, composed by unknown authors, were usually written down. Little by little they were changed by the people who sang them. Sometimes stanzas were added, changed or left out completely. It is not unusual to find several versions of the same ballad each with a somewhat different story to tell.

A beautiful and haunting medieval ballad, "Lord Randal," is printed on the following page. In it two people are speaking, a mother and her son. In the first two lines of each stanza (except the sixth) the mother asks her son a question; his answer to her appears in the last two lines of each stanza.

This ballad can be read by one person or two, one reading the mother's lines, another the son's. When reading "Lord Randal," notice that the last word in the third line of each stanza is *soon.* The last word in the fourth line of each stanza is *down. Down* should be pronounced as *doon* to rhyme with *soon.* Also check the footnotes before reading for better understanding of the old English terms.

After you have finished reading the ballad, answer the questions below.

1. Do you think Lord Randal was a wealthy man? Why or why not? _____
    _____

2. Does the ballad tell us why Lord Randal was murdered? _____

3. How was Lord Randal murdered? _____

4. Who murdered him? _____

5. When did Lord Randal's mother know that he was poisoned? _____
    _____

6. When in the ballad did you get the feeling that Lord Randal's mother was suspicious

    of his illness? _____

7. The last four stanzas are concerned with what kind of practical matter? _____

8. What did Lord Randal leave his "true-love"? _____

9. Rewrite the story of Lord Randal in modern dialogue and setting but keep the spirit and story of the ballad.

10. "Lord Randal" is a story of love and tragedy. Compare it to Shakespeare's *Romeo and Juliet.*

11. Compare "Lord Randal" to a modern movie, play or musical which has a similar theme.

12. If you enjoyed reading "Lord Randal," read the medieval ballad called "Barbara Allan."

Lord Randal

"O where ha you been, Lord Randal, my son?
And where ha you been, my handsome young man?"
"I ha been at the greenwood; mother, mak my bed soon,
For I'm wearied wi hunting, and fain wad lie down."

"An wha met ye there, Lord Randal, my son?
An wha met you there, my handsome young man?"
"O I met wi my true-love; mother, mak my bed soon,
For I'm wearied wi huntin, an fain wad lie down."

"And what did she give you, Lord Randal, my son?
And what did she give you, my handsome young man?"
"Eels fried in a pan; mother, mak my bed soon,
For I'm wearied wi huntin, and fain wad lie down."

"And wha gat your leavins, Lord Randal, my son?
And wha gat your leavins, my handsome young man?"
"My hawks and my hounds; mother, mak my bed soon,
For I'm wearied wi hunting, and fain wad lie down."

"And what becam of them, Lord Randal, my son?
And what becam of them, my handsome young man?"
"They stretched their legs out an died; mother, mak my bed soon,
For I'm wearied wi huntin, and fain wad lie down."

"O I fear you are poisoned, Lord Randal, my son!
I fear you are poisoned, my handsome young man!"
"O yes, I am poisoned; mother, mak my bed soon,
For I'm sick at the heart, and I fain wad lie down."

"What d'ye leave to your mother, Lord Randal, my son?
What d'ye leave to your mother, my handsome young man?"
"Four and twenty milk kye; mother, mak my bed soon,
For I'm sick at the heart, and I fain wad lie down."

"What'd ye leave to your sister, Lord Randal, my son?
What d'ye leave to your sister, my handsome young man?"
"My gold and my silver; mother, mak my bed soon.
For I'm sick at the heart, and I fain wad lie down."

"What d'ye leave to your brother, Lord Randal, my son?
What d'ye leave to your brother, my handsome young man?"
"My houses and my lands; mother, mak my bed soon,
For I'm sick at the heart, and I fain wad lie down."

"What d'ye leave to your true-love, Lord Randal, my son?
What d'ye leave to your true-love, my handsome young man?"
"I leave her hell and fire; mother, mak my bed soon,
For I'm sick at the heart, and I fain wad lie down."

Line 3 - *greenwood* means *the forest.*
Line 4 - *fain* means *gladly*
Line 7 - *true-love* means *sweetheart, fiancee.*
Line 11 - *eels* are fish with snakelike bodies.
Line 13 - *"Gat your leavins"* means *got the leftover scraps of food.*
Line 27 - *kye* means *cows.*

Mind Your Manors

The manorial system was built around the lord, his lands, the peasants who worked for the lord and the main house or manor. The manor, which was often a castle, served as the heart of the manorial system. The purpose of the manorial system was to be a self-sufficient community. In order to do this the lands of the manor covered hundreds and sometimes thousands of acres. This land was used for farming, pasture for animals, hunting and for timber. The part of the land on which the manor house itself was built was called the lord's demesne (pronounced *di-mane*). Nearby were the stables, barns, a bakehouse, cookhouse and sometimes a windmill. There was also a chapel and rectory or priest's house a short distance away.

Everything that was needed for life was produced on the manor. From the fields came the main crops of grains, such as wheat or rye, as bread was the staff of life. The forests provided game. In most cases, however, the peasants were allowed to kill only small animals, such as rabbits. Deer and other species of larger game were reserved for the lord and his family, as hunting was as much a way of entertaining as it was a necessity.

Most of the farm animals were slaughtered in the fall since more often than not there was not enough food to feed them over the winter. The main beverages were beer, wine or cider, as water was not always fit for drinking and most of the milk was made into cheese.

The peasants of the Middle Ages were called serfs. They did most of the work on the land of the lord in exchange for protection and a right to live on the manor. They were considered to be part of the lord's property and ranked little above his sheep and cattle. A small number of people called freemen rented land from the lord and could leave the manor. Serfs could not.

Many serfs spent their entire lives without ever leaving the manor on which they were born. The years of their lives passed, each one as the one before it. The monotony of a serf's life was broken only by war, church holidays, hunting, and athletic contests.

Discussion Questions:
1. The son of a serf had very few opportunities to escape becoming a serf and leading a life of hard work and drudgery as his father and grandfather before him. Discuss the opportunities available today for rising above one's station in life.
2. Contrast the life of a nobleman's son or daughter to that of a serf's.

Mind Your Manors

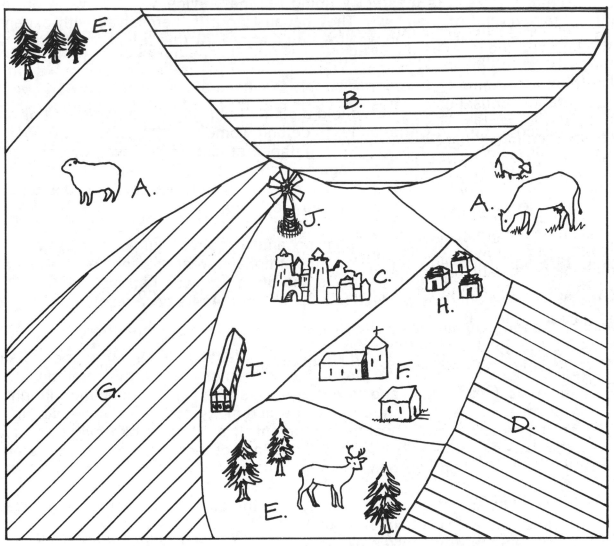

Use letters to match the parts of a manor to the descriptions below.

1._____ the fortified house of the lord, called the manor

2._____ the forest or land used for hunting

3._____ the west field

4._____ pasture land for animals

5._____ the barns, stables, bakehouse and cookhouse

6._____ serfs' or peasants' huts

7._____ east field

8._____ the windmill which was used for grinding grain

9._____ the chapel and rectory

10._____ the north field

Knighthood

In the year 1066, the Normans conquered England. These French soldiers who came on horseback were called knights by the English. Later, any man who could fight on horseback came to be known as a knight. When not fighting or going about the business of war, a knight served his master by doing routine service. As time wore on many knights obtained land of their own. They began to outfit themselves with expensive weapons and armor that only the wealthy could afford. At this time only the rich were considered to be knights, but any man could be made a knight for deeds of honor or distinction.

Early medieval knights swore to uphold a code of chivalry. In the code of chivalry a knight promised to uphold Christianity, to defend women and to protect the poor and the weak. A boy started on his way to knighthood at about age seven by becoming a page in the household of a lord. As a page he learned to ride a horse, received religious training, was taught manners, hunting, dancing and possibly learned to read and write if there was someone in the manor who could teach him.

At about age twelve or thirteen the page became a squire. Squires were assistants to the knights. A squire looked after the knight's armor and weapons and became skilled in their use. He served the knight his meals and often followed him into battle. In tournaments he was the only one allowed to help a knight. As he became older he engaged in tournaments himself.

The night before a squire became a knight he confessed his sins to a priest, bathed and fasted. Dressed all in white he prayed the entire night before the ceremony. In the morning the priest blessed him, and he was asked his reasons for becoming a knight. He was then given a new suit of armor; and in a ceremony called an accolade, he was stroked on the shoulder, thus becoming a knight. If a knight broke his vows or was dishonorable, he was stripped of his knighthood in another ceremony which pretended to bury him, for in the Middle Ages, "a knight without honor is no longer alive."

By the year 1200, knights were much aware of the differences between themselves and others, and a definite class of aristocratic knights developed. They owned land and castles, they identified themselves by family crests and passed on their titles to their sons. Distinct lines were drawn between those who had wealth and power and those who did not. These lines became sharper as a result of the exposure of knights to the riches of the East in their travels during the Crusades. Knights now desired luxuries in their castles, silk and jewels to wear, and spices and sugar in their diets. Knighthood had changed. No one will ever know how many medieval men lived to be perfect knights, but the ideal of chivalry—loyalty, courtesy, courage, truth and above all, honor—set the standards for the Middle Ages and for all the Ages that followed.

In modern times knighthood is inherited, or it can be an honor bestowed by a monarch in order to recognize outstanding service to one's country. A knight is referred to by the title of Sir. The wife of a knight is called a Lady. A woman who is knighted is called Dame.

1. Medieval knights took an oath of chivalry. What has the word *chivalry* come to mean in today's world?
2. Are the qualities of loyalty, courtesy, courage, truth and honor still valued? Explain your answer.
3. Write a code for living in modern times.

Knighthood

Each of the drawings below is associated with knighthood. After you have read the descriptions, tell which stage—page, squire or knight—is being described. Finally, give the logical order of the stages as depicted in the drawings.

1. In battle he was at his lord's side always ready to assist him in his needs. __

2. The night before he became a knight he confessed his sins, fasted and prayed. _____

3. He began to learn to ride early in life if he were to become a knight. _____

4. A touch of the blade of a sword in a ceremony, called the accolade, made him a knight. _____

5. He had his own armor and weapons and had sworn to a code of chivalry. _____

6. Learning to hunt and hunting with falcons was an important part of his training. _____

The early medieval legend of King Arthur, his knights, and his queen Guinevere is one of the oldest and best loved in the English language. You may wish to read more about this legend from books in your school or town library or from the following sources:

Barber, Richard. *King Arthur in Legend and History (Rowman, 1974).*

Hibbert, Christopher and Thomas, Charles. *The Search for King Arthur* (American Heritage, 1970).

Lanier, Sidney. *The Boy's King Arthur* (Scribner, 1973).

Picard, B. L. *Stories of King Arthur and His Knights* (Walck, 1955).

Armor

Suits of armor used to protect the body in times of war or combat go back thousands of years. It was, however, during the Middle Ages that armor reached its highest point and also its decline. In the early Middle Ages armor consisted of a helmet and hauberk, a kind of shirt made of chain mail, which protected the body from the neck to the knees. The invention of the crossbow made the armor of chain mail ineffective, and a suit of metal plates was added. In time the entire body was encased in a suit of armor. Armor was very expensive and was worn only by knights and sometimes squires. Common soldiers, being horseless, did not wear heavy armor. They wore instead those pieces they found on the battlefield, provided that they were not too heavy. Sometimes foot soldiers wore steel caps and shirts of mail.

In time, armor became so complicated that it took two men to dress a knight. A suit of armor was made up of a number of small steel plates strapped onto the knight's body. The large number of plates was necessary to enable the knight to move as freely as possible. After the main pieces were in place, the smaller pieces were attached by hooks and buckles. Because knights in armor were dressed for combat on horses, the horses too were outfitted with armor, lest they be killed, leaving the knight almost defenseless.

Although armor was used well into the seventeenth century, its use declined rapidly as military tactics changed, demanding rapid movement; and the use of gunpowder became widespread. Today suits of ancient armor can only be seen in museums and such places, but modern day soldiers still wear helmets for protection and policemen sometimes wear bulletproof vests, two items of bodily protection originally invented many centuries ago.

Armor

Match the parts of a suit of armor on the following page to the descriptions below by placing the correct letters in the numbered spaces.

1._____ *Helmet* (hell-met). The headpiece or head covering in a suit of armor.

2._____ *Cuisse* (kwis). This word is taken from the Latin word *coxa,* meaning *hip.* It is the piece of armor that covers the thigh.

3._____ *Greave* (greeve). This term comes from the Old French word *greve,* which refers to the part in the hair. It is the part of the armor that protects the leg from the ankle to the knee.

4._____ *Gauntlet* (gont-let). This word comes from the Old French word *gant,* which means *glove.* Gauntlets were the armor gloves that protected the hands.

5._____ *Coat of mail* (male). Taken from the Latin word *maculata,* which means *spotty, mesh* or *net,* it refers to a coat made of metal rings or links which was worn under the armor.

6._____ *Visor* (vi-zer). The moveable part of the helmet in front of the eyes. It comes from the French word for face, *vis.*

7._____ *Shoulder piece.*

8._____ *Elbow piece.*

9._____ *Knee piece.*

10._____ *Gorget* (gor-jet). A piece of armor that protects the throat. It comes from an Old French word *gorge,* meaning *throat.*

11._____ *Tasse* (tass). This term comes from the Old French word *tasse,* which means *pocket.* It is a series of overlapping plates which together form a short skirt.

12._____ *Cuirass* (kwi-ras). A breast plate from the neck to the waist. It was originally made of leather and comes from a Latin word *corium,* which means *leather.*

13._____ *Sabaton* (sab-a-ton). Taken from the French word *sabot,* a wooden shoe. It is the part of a suit of armor that covers the foot.

14._____ *Brassard* (bras-sard). This is the armor that protects the arm. Brassard comes from the Latin word *bracchium,* which means *arm.*

Armor

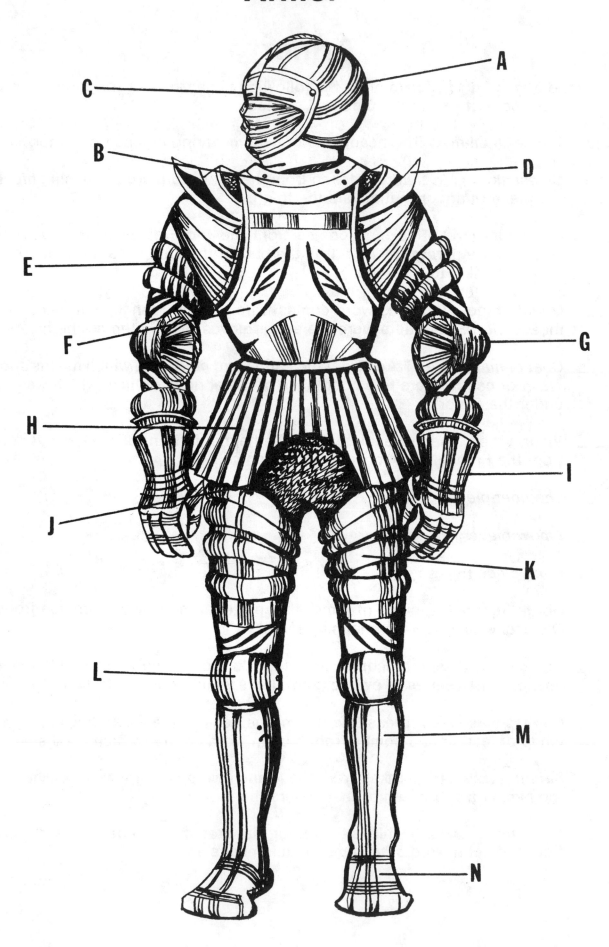

Weaponry of the Middle Ages

The weapons of the Middle Ages are very different from those used by today's soldiers. Wars were often scenes of brutal, hand-to-hand fighting. The knights did their fighting protected by heavy suits of armor and riding on horseback, while foot soldiers used bows and arrows or fought hand to hand with crude weapons and wore little protection from the blows of their enemies.

Weapons of the Middle Ages are drawn on the following page. How many of them can you match to their names below?

1._____ a lance, which was a type of spear carried by knights.

2._____ a long bow and arrow, used by foot soldiers.

3._____ a mace was used for clubbing. It was usually carried by foot soldiers. It had a ball with spikes attached to a wooden handle.

4._____ a dagger.

5._____ a battle-axe, a weapon of foot soldiers.

6._____ a crossbow and arrow, a powerful and accurate weapon.

7._____ a sword, usually carried by a knight, sometimes by foot soldiers.

8._____ a scabbard, the cover or shield for the sword.

9._____ a halberd, a combination of a battle-axe and a pike. It was about six feet long and was usually the weapon of a knight.

10._____ a bludgeon, a type of mace, carried by foot soldiers. It was used like a club with the ball attached to the club by a chain.

11._____ a war hammer or hawk's beak, so named for its shape. It was used to pierce mail.

12._____ a mace, made with bars of spikes attached to a handle. Used by foot soldiers for clubbing.

Weaponry of the Middle Ages

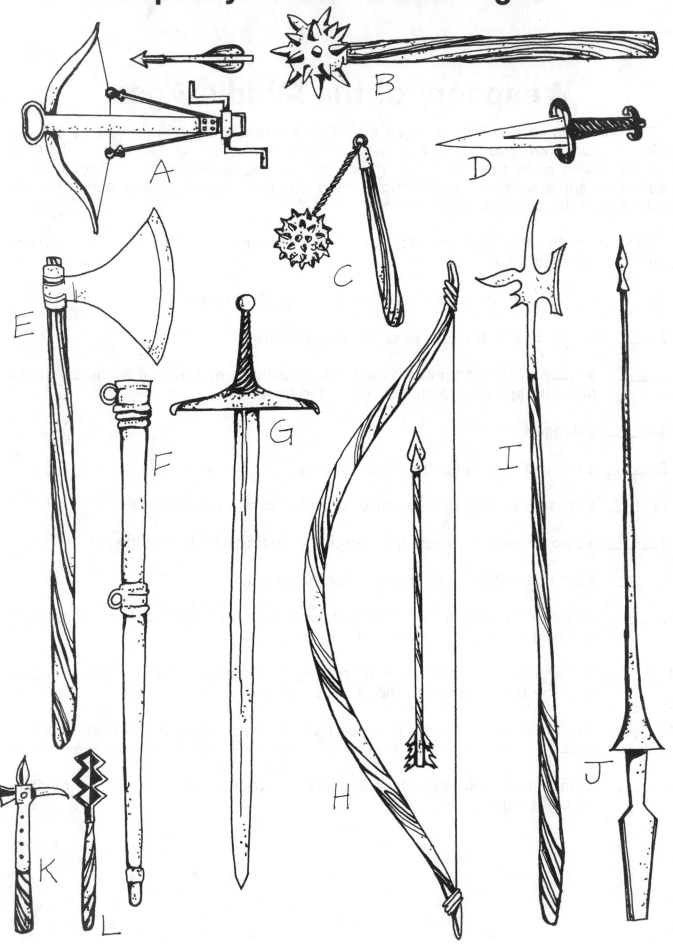

The Order of the Garter

Great Britain's highest order of knighthood is known by an unusual name, the Order of the Garter. An old legend has it that a certain king of England, King Edward III, in the year 1349 A.D. was dancing at a ball with a beautiful countess. While they were dancing, her blue garter fell to the floor. The gallant king picked up the garter and returned it to the countess. Several people at the ball noticed this act, and they began to smile and whisper. King Edward III became angry and said in French, "Honi soit qui mal y pense," which means "Evil be to him who evil thinks."

A short time later Edward decided to make the blue garter a coveted symbol so that everyone would wish to wear it. He began the Order of the Garter in 1349 and proposed for its emblem a blue garter with the words "Honi soit qui mal y pense" printed on it. Today the Order of the Garter is limited to very few people. They are usually members of the royal family of Great Britain or other foreign rulers. It has been over six hundred years since King Edward III picked up the little blue garter of the countess. She herself has long been forgotten, but the deed is still remembered; and the Order of the Garter, just as King Edward wished it to be, is one of the most desired awards in the world.

The next time you see a formal portrait of the present queen of England, Queen Elizabeth II, she may be wearing a blue ribbon diagonally across her chest. This blue ribbon with its badge tells us that she belongs to the Order of the Garter. Winston Churchill, former Prime Minister of Great Britain and leader of the English nation during World War II, was also a member of the Order of the Garter. It was his most treasured award and was publicly displayed at his funeral according to his wishes.

The United States does not have an award that closely resembles the Order of the Garter. Why do you think this is so?

Many countries, including the United States, give other awards for outstanding service. On the next page seven famous awards are listed. Use an encyclopedia to find out which country gives each award, why it is given and whether it is a military or civilian (nonmilitary) honor.

Decorations and Awards

Award	Country	Why Given?	Military or Civilian Honor?
Congressional Medal of Honor			
Order of the Purple Heart			
Iron Cross			
Presidential Medal of Freedom			
Croix de Guerre			
Victoria Cross			
Legion of Honor			

A Thirteenth Century Noblewoman's Costume

A noblewoman living in the thirteenth century wore a full-length gown which was loosely fitted and often set off by a narrow belt. Around the neck the *gown* might have been decorated with embroidery or fur. A sleeveless coat, called a *cyclas,* was worn over the gown. The cyclas was a garment worn by both men and women. In cold weather a cape, called a *mantle,* was worn over the shoulders fastened at the neck by a cord.

Perhaps the most important parts of her costume to a thirteenth century noblewoman were her headdress and hairdress. One kind of headdress popular at the time consisted of a pillbox hat which was called a *coif.* The coif was worn over a chin band or *barbette.* The barbette fastened at the top of the head under the hat. The coif and barbette were usually white. To hold her hair, the noblewoman used a net called a *crespine.* The crespine was usually in color or of gold.

Shoes were plain and in dark colors with pointed toes. Sometimes they were fastened with laces. *Stockings* were striped.

Although thirteenth century clothes were generally plain, they were colorful. The noblewoman's gown on the next page could possibly have been green, blue or purple; her cyclas might have been red and her mantle still another color.

Activities:
1. Use the italicized terms above to label the parts of the noblewoman's costume on the next page.
2. Color the costume by using some of the suggestions for colors given above or you may wish to cut out the figure and paste it on cardboard. Use scraps of felt or other materials cut to fit the articles of clothing shown. Attach the material to the figure with glue.
3. Names as well as costumes "go in and out of style." Eleanor, Matilda, Blanche, Elizabeth, Emma, Ann, Isabelle, and Helen were favorite names for girls about a thousand years ago. Take a poll in your class to find out how many girls have names that lasted.
4. Louis, Philip, Henry, William, Charles, Robert, John, and Edward were popular names for boys during the Middle Ages. Take a poll in your class to find out how many boys have names that lasted.

A Thirteenth Century Noblewoman's Costume

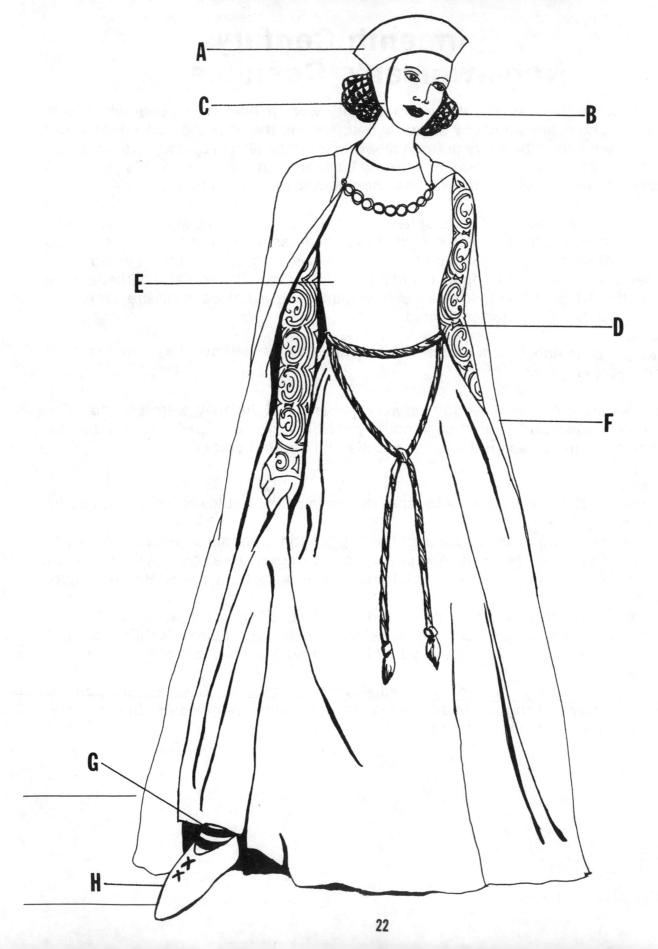

How to Make a Hennin

No one knows exactly where the word *hennin* came from or how it got its meaning. Some scholars think that it may have been a term shouted as an insult at the women who wore these tall hats by other women who could not afford them. As time went on the term came to mean *a tall cone-shaped hat.* These hats were worn by noblewomen during the late Middle Ages.

Hennins became the fashion rage of the late fifteenth century. They often had veils or scarfs attached to them and were sometimes referred to as steeple hats. It was said that castle doorways had to be made taller in order that women wearing these headdresses could pass through without losing them.

Materials: cardboard paper or sheet of oaktag about 22 inches tall and 26 inches wide, scissors, tape and stapler

Procedure: Follow the steps below.

Step #1

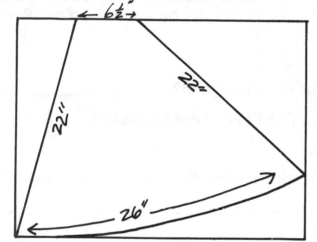

1. Make a pattern as shown above.

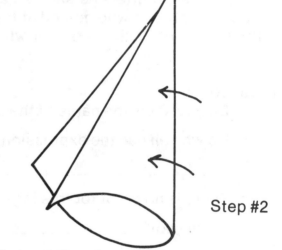

Step #2

2. Cut out the shape of the hat and twist into a cone. Try out base for head size. Staple or tape securely.

Step #3

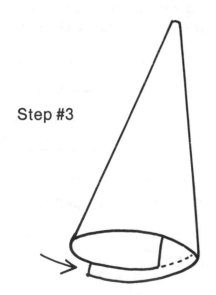

3. Trim the base of the hat.

Step #4

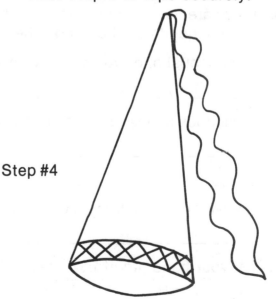

4. Decorate with veil and trim.

A Famous Legend

In the eleventh century there was a beautiful noblewoman who lived with her husband in Coventry, England. This noblewoman with long blond hair that reached almost to the floor was noted as much for her goodness as for her beauty. Her husband, Lord Leofric of Mercia, was not nearly as good as she. The taxes he levied on his people were so heavy that many were not able to pay them. His wife often pleaded with him to reduce them, but he would not. One day while she was asking him to help the poor people, he laughed and said, "Only if you'll ride throughout the streets of town naked." Of course Lord Leofric knew his wife was a very modest woman, and he did not expect her to accept his offer, but angry as she was with her husband, she did. The beautiful wife told all the townspeople to close their shutters and remain inside and she would do as her husband asked. The legend goes on to say that everyone in Coventry stayed inside and locked their shutters as she had asked, except the local tailor, a man named Tom. Tom was the only one who peered at the lady with the long blond hair as she rode throughout the streets of Coventry on her white horse, and forever after he was known as "Peeping Tom."

Questions:

1. Do you know the name of the Lady in this famous legend? _____

2. Do we still use the expression, "Peeping Tom?" What does it mean? _____
_____

3. There is no proof for this legend; do you think it could have actually happened? Why
or why not? _____
_____
_____

4. There are many other legends in history which cannot be proven true or false. Many times legends are based on the lives of real people as in the case of Lady Godiva and her husband. Do you know of at least two other legends? _____
_____

5. What does it mean to be a "living legend"? _____
_____
_____

6. How might a well-known political figure or entertainer of today become a legend? __
_____

7. Try your hand at writing a legend about someone you admire.

Communication by Letter

There were only two ways of communicating during the medieval times. One was by way of mouth, the other was by letter writing. Letters were written on parchment, which is the skin of a sheep or goat. The parchment was prepared by first thoroughly washing the skin and then scraping away all the hair. Then the skin was rewashed and stretched on frames to dry. After drying, it was scraped again and rubbed with chalk and pumice to make it soft, smooth and shiny. Lastly it was cut and folded. If the parchment was to be used in a book, it was folded and sewn together.

If a lord wished to send a letter, he would use a piece of parchment, ink made from soot and a dried goose feather for a pen. Many times he would hire a scribe to write his letters for him. When the letter was finished, the parchment was rolled or folded, tied with a cord and sealed with wax. The lord then pressed his identification to the warm wax. The wax seal told the receiver whether or not the letter had been opened. The personal seal also showed that the letter had not been forged, a very important precaution in times of treachery and war.

Pretend you are a knight or a lady living in the Middle Ages. You wish to write a letter to your brother who is a monk. You may wish to invite him to visit; tell him some news of your life in the castle, report how his nieces or nephews are getting along, or perhaps write about your concern of danger such as an approaching attack or a widespread disease. Follow the directions on the next page for sealing your letter.

Variation: Classmates may wish to exchange letters.

Communication by Letter

Materials: sealing wax or candle, matches, writing paper, cord (optional), and seal

1. Roll or fold your letter.

2. Tie it with a cord or ribbon if you wish.

3. If sealing wax is available, use it as it works best. Seal your letter by first lighting a candle and allowing a mound of wax the size of a quarter to collect on the seam of the letter. When the wax begins to cool and has formed a soft crust, press your personal seal into the wax. Your special seal can be that of a ring or another piece of jewelry, a button or some other appropriate object.

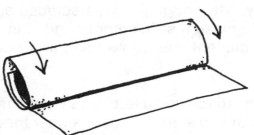

Caution: This activity should only be done with responsible students under the direction of an adult.

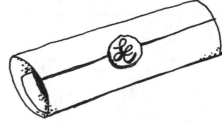

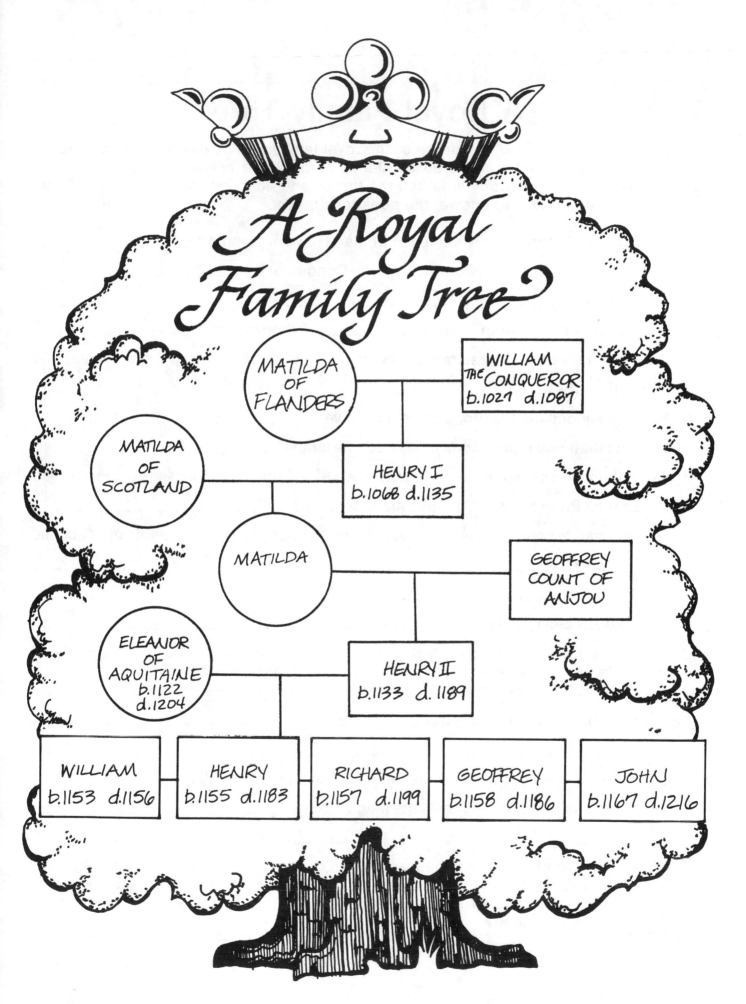

A Royal Family Tree

MATILDA OF FLANDERS

WILLIAM THE CONQUEROR b.1027 d.1087

MATILDA OF SCOTLAND

HENRY I b.1068 d.1135

MATILDA

GEOFFREY COUNT OF ANJOU

ELEANOR OF AQUITAINE b.1122 d.1204

HENRY II b.1133 d.1189

WILLIAM b.1153 d.1156

HENRY b.1155 d.1183

RICHARD b.1157 d.1199

GEOFFREY b.1158 d.1186

JOHN b.1167 d.1216

A Royal Family Tree

On the preceding page is a portion of the royal family tree of William the Conqueror. For the sake of simplicity, some descendents' names have been omitted and in most cases only those who directly inherited the throne and their spouses are shown. Study the royal tree and use it to answer the questions below.

1. What name did three noblewomen of England have in common? _____

2. Who inherited the throne from William the Conqueror? _____

3. Did Henry I have a male heir? _____

4. Who was the daughter of Henry I? _____ Whom did she marry? _____

5. When Eleanor of Aquitaine married Henry II, he was the Count of Anjou. Where did he get that title? _____

6. How many sons did Eleanor and Henry II have? _____

7. Why did their two oldest sons never become kings? _____

8. Their third son became famous as the leader of the Third Crusade. He was also called the Lion-Hearted. What was his first name? _____

9. Richard had no children. When he died why did not his brother, Geoffrey, succeed him? _____

   _____

   Who did succeed Richard? _____

10. The youngest son of Henry II and Eleanor of Aquitaine was called "John Lackland" by his father when he was born. What do you think his father meant when he referred to his son as Lackland? (Hint: Remember he was the fifth son.) Why did John's father turn out to be wrong? _____

    _____

11. John was a very mean ruler for the English people, and in 1215 his barons forced him to sign the Magna Carta. What is the Magna Carta? _____

    _____

12. Eleanor of Aquitaine's first husband was Louis VII of France. She was the only woman in history to have been Queen of both France and England. Altogether she had ten children; two of her daughters became queens. How many of her sons became English kings?

Your Family Tree

You may wish to make a family tree of your own. Ask your parents, grandparents, aunts and uncles for help. The study of your ancestors is called genealogy. Many people study genealogy as a hobby.

Family Tree

"The Perfect Knight"

Richard I was the third son of Henry II of England and his wife Eleanor of Aquitaine. As his mother's favorite, he was raised according to her ideals of a perfect knight. At the age of eleven he was given the duchy of Aquitaine, his mother's inheritance. As a young man he distinguished himself in military tactics and knightly skills. That he was courageous beyond belief and a true leader of men there could be no doubt, and for these reasons he was called Richard Coeur de Lion, or Richard the Lion-Hearted. For his heroism he was widely praised in the ballads sung by the troubadours of his time.

After his brother's death, Richard became heir to the throne of England. Unfortunately Henry II had a favorite son also; it was Richard's younger brother, John. It was Henry's wish to bypass Richard and leave the throne to John. Richard joined forces with Phillip II, King of France, against his father and eventually forced Henry to recognize him as his heir.

After Richard was crowned monarch, he became interested in the Crusades and proved himself to be the ablest leader of the Third Crusade. In this Crusade he was able to obtain certain rights for Christians from the Turkish ruler, Saladin. Returning from the Holy Land, Richard was captured. He was later released for a very large ransom.

Richard spent the last five years of his life warring against his once ally, Phillip II of France. Over and over again Richard proved to be the better warrior. It was however during a truce with Phillip that Richard was mortally wounded. A young peasant, standing on a castle wall and using a frying pan for a shield, spotted Richard talking to his knights below. He aimed his crossbow and expertly released the arrow striking Richard in the back. The archer was promptly captured and brought to the dying king. "What harm have I done to you that you have killed me?" Richard asked. "You once slew my father and my brother. Take what revenge you like," answered the proud young man. "Go in peace." Richard gave the command to release the prisoner, and in death as so many times in life, he showed himself to be the "perfect knight." Richard at his own request was buried at the feet of his father with whom he so often quarreled.

Choose one of the following personalities or choose someone from the Middle Ages and write a short biographical sketch about your selection.

Charlemagne	William the Conqueror	Henry II of England
Eleanor of Aquitaine	Richard the Lion-Hearted	Blanche of Castile
Thomas Aquinas	Louis IX of France	

A Crusader's Helmet

To make a model of a knight's helmet similar to the kind King Richard the Lion-Hearted may have worn in the Third Crusade, follow the directions below.

Materials: strong but flexible paper, scissors, pencils, yardstick, X-acto knife or single-edged razor blade, gold paint and plumes (optional)

Procedure: Draw the helmet according to the dimensions given below. With scissors or X-acto knife cut out the helmet, making one-inch-wide strips at the top.

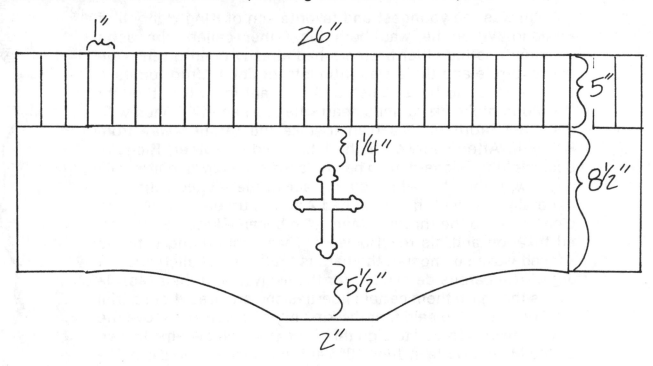

Next use the knife or razor blade to cut out the design for the eyes and nose.

Staple the helmet along the 8½-inch margin to make a cylinder as in A. Beginning at the back, gently and neatly fold the one-inch strips one over the other as in B. Fasten the strips at the top with a stapler or paper clip. Spray-paint the helmet gold or silver. Allow to dry. Add plumes to give your helmet a festive touch as shown in drawing C. Many helmets had visors which could be raised or lowered over the face. If you make a helmet with a visor, use paper clips for attaching the visor to the helmet. Clean, three-gallon, cylindrical ice-cream containers from ice-cream parlors also make nice helmets.

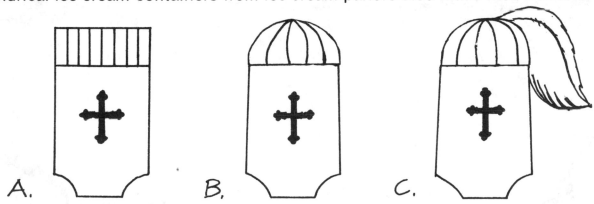

A.　　　B.　　　C.

King John and the Magna Carta

John was the youngest and favorite son of King Henry II of England. When he was born his father called him John Lackland, as his older brothers had already been given large lands to rule and there was little left for John. Unfortunately, John grew up to be a selfish and arrogant man. It is thought that John broke his father's heart when he secretly joined with his older brothers in a plan to take the throne away from Henry II. After Henry's death, John's older brother, Richard, became king. Richard, who had no sons of his own, named his nephew, Arthur, to be his heir in place of the wicked John. It is generally believed that John had Arthur murdered, giving him clear claim to the throne. When John became king he increased taxation and his royal powers. These acts along with his wicked ways so angered the barons that they rebelled against John. The barons demanded for themselves and their vassals rights that gave them certain liberties and ensured them a trial by jury. They also said that the king himself was not above the law. John was forced to sign this charter which became known as the Magna Carta in June 1215 at Runnymede, a field outside of London. King John died a year later reportedly after overindulging in a meal of peaches and beer.

Pretend that you are a baron in King John's time. Prepare a charter in which you and the other barons would demand certain rights for yourselves and your vassals who have been denied many of the freedoms we enjoy today. To make your document look ancient, follow the suggestions on the next page.

Aging Documents

You can make an important paper or document "age" instantly by following the simple procedures outlined below.

Materials: white, tan or grey construction paper, tea bag, hot water, cup, candle, sponge, calligraphy pen (optional)

Procedure:
1. Make a strong solution of one tea bag in ½ cup of hot water.

2. Dip a corner of the sponge in the strong tea and wipe over the paper to stain it.

3. Tear the edges of the paper in several places. Make the tears ½ to 1-inch deep.

4. Over a sink carefully use a lighted candle to singe the edges of the paper. If the paper begins to flame, use the sponge to smother it or drop it in the sink.

5. Allow the paper to dry.

6. If a calligraphy pen is available, use it to write your message.

1 + 1 = WHO?

Read the blocks from left to right. There are two hints to the identity of a famous person of the Middle Ages in the blocks. Write the name of the person described in the block at the right.

Wicked King of England	+	Signed the Magna Carta	=	
Married Matilda of Flanders	+	Victor at the Battle of Hastings	=	
Known in French as Coeur de Lion	+	Leader of the Third Crusade	=	
Helped lower taxes in Coventry	+	Rode naked on a white horse	=	
His grandsons divided his kingdom	+	Emperor of the Holy Roman Empire	=	
Count of Anjou	+	Father of Henry II	=	
English King and Leader of Saxons	+	Defeated and killed at Battle of Hastings	=	
Turkish ruler	+	Granted Christians privileges after Third Crusade	=	
Wife of Henry II	+	Was once Queen of France and England	=	
English King who liked to dance	+	Made the Order of the Garter a special honor	=	

34

A Royal Crown

A favorite design of French and English royalty during the Middle Ages is known as the fleur-de-lis (pronounced flur-duh-lee). It means flower of light and represents the iris flower. It was widely used in heraldry, on royal garments and as a design on crowns. To make a crown similar to those worn in the Middle Ages, follow the instructions below.

Materials: strong but flexible cardboard type paper or poster board, gold spray paint, magic markers, sequins, false gems or pearls, ruler, pencil, glue, needle and thread or stapler

Procedure:

1. Use a ruler to mark off twenty-four inches on the edge of your paper.

2. Cut out fleur-de-lis design to use as a pattern for your crown.

3. Leave a two-inch tab on the left side of paper for fitting and stapling. Begin tracing pattern at the two-inch mark and repeat five times. There will be a leftover tab on the right side, also.

4. Cut out the crown. Spray gold or color with magic markers. Allow to dry overnight. Decorate with false gems, sequins, pearls, etc. Adjust to head size and sew or staple the band at the tabs.

Heraldry

Heraldry began as badges of recognition. The symbols which are called charges were first painted on the shields of knights during the twelfth century. The custom spread during the Crusades and became popular in tournaments where knights, unrecognizable in full armor, gathered to fight. In time, combinations of symbols came to be known as a family's coat of arms. Coats of arms to this day are handed down from father to son.

Lions were a favorite charge in English heraldry, while fleur-de-lis were popular in France. Other popular charges were eagles, unicorns, dragons, along with a variety of birds, fish, seashells, leaves, trees, and flowers. Inanimate objects such as castles, towers, tools, keys and musical instruments were also used.

Heraldry had a practical side, also. Popular during a period of history when leaders in battle could not be identified because of their armor, the symbols on their shields made them recognizable. Coats of arms displayed on flags or banners from a nobleman's castle were used to indicate that he was in residence, and in death his coat of arms often marked his tomb. Coats of arms were also carved into rings. This symbol when pressed into soft wax was used almost as a signature for identification purposes and as a seal for documents. The French did much in organizing the science of heraldry, and the standard colors used in heraldry are known by their Old French names. The names of the seven colors, called tinctures, used in heraldry are: *argent* for white or silver, *or* for gold, *azure* for blue, *gules* for red, *sable* for black, *vert* for green, and *purpure* for purple. There are also two fur patterns, *ermine* and *vair*.

Heraldry

The first divisions of a shield are as shown below.

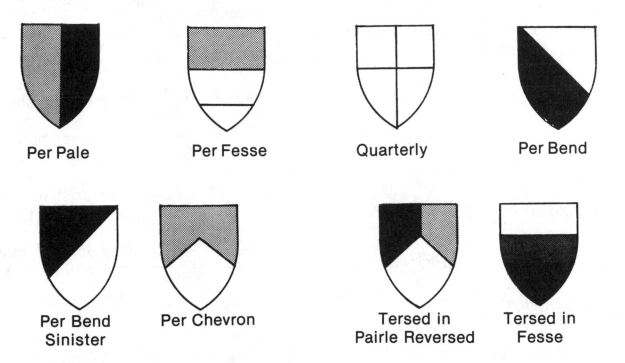

Per Pale   Per Fesse   Quarterly   Per Bend

Per Bend Sinister   Per Chevron   Tersed in Pairle Reversed   Tersed in Fesse

Shields are divided further. The second divisions are called ordinaries. Ordinaries can be divided again into subordinaries; only the ordinaries and their names are given below.

Chief   Filet   Fesse   Pale   Bend   Bend Sinister

Chevron   Cross   Saltire   Pile   Pall or Shakefork

Decorating the Shield

Shields were handed down from fathers to sons. To show the order of births of the sons of a family, the shield was marked by a symbol such as the ones shown below. These symbols are called marks of cadency. Marks of cadency were important in order to distinguish the sons of the same family because only the oldest son inherited the original coat of arms, the castle or manor and the land which went with it. If you are a son, you may wish to make your shield more individualized by adding a mark of cadency to show your order of birth.

The file or label, mark of the oldest son

The crescent, mark of the second son

The mullet, mark of the third son

The martlet, mark of the fourth son

The annulet, mark of the fifth son

The fleur-de-lis, mark of the sixth son

The rose, mark of the seventh son

The cross moline, mark of the eighth son

The octofoil, mark of the ninth son

Marks of Cadency

Lions were an early and favorite charge or symbol of English heraldry. They were used on shields and as supporters in coats of arms. The lions as well as other animals were usually depicted in one of the four positions shown below. Use the descriptions at the bottom of the page to identify and label the drawings below.

_____ _____ _____ _____

1. Passant—from the Old French word *passer,* to pass. It refers to an animal walking with its more distant forepaw raised.
2. Couchant—from the Old French word *coucher,* to couch. It refers to an animal lying down with its head raised.
3. Rampant—from an Old French word *ramper,* to climb. It refers to an animal rearing on its hind feet ready to climb.
4. Statant—from the Latin *stare,* to stand. It refers to an animal standing.

Design a Heraldric Shield

As you can see heraldry is a complicated art which uses many technical terms. It is also governed by strict sets of rules. You can pretend to go back in time when heraldry was much less complicated and design your own shield as did Richard I, who used lions as a symbol of his courage, or as a family named Griffin, who hundreds of years ago selected the mythical animal, the griffon, in a clever play on words. Cut out and trace this outline on another sheet of paper to make your own or your family's shield. The divisions, ordinaries and colors discussed on the preceding pages will help you to conform to some of the basic rules of heraldry.

A Royal Coat of Arms

A royal coat of arms consists of the parts shown on the next page. The complete combination of the shield, helmet, crest and motto is known as the achievement. See if you can match the names and descriptions of the parts of a coat of arms to the letters on page 41.

1._____ Helmets come in a wide variety of shapes depending on the country and time of the origin of the coat of arms. In heraldry the helmet always faces left (to the right of the shield itself). Only the helmets of kings and nobility are depicted full face.

2._____ Supporters are real or mythological animals supporting the shield with their feet resting on the scroll. They were introduced into heraldry in the fourteenth century. They are usually reserved for kings and other nobility.

3._____ Crests also made their appearance in the fourteenth century. They were usually made of a lightweight material such as light wood or leather and were worn on the top of knights' helmets.

4._____ The mantle gets its name from the French word *manteau.* A silk mantle was used by a knight to shade the back of his helmet from the sun.

5._____ Scrolls had mottos written on them. The motto might be one word or a sentence. It is generally believed that the motto began as a battle or war cry.

6._____ The wreath consisted of two pieces of colored silk twisted together. It always shows six twists in the same colors as the shield. It may be curved or straight.

7._____ The shield may vary in shape. Usually it is a rectangle with a pointed or curved base which comes to a point. Emblems or charges of heraldry are shown on the shield. Crosses were often used during the time of the Crusades.

Many family names have a coat of arms. Most libraries have books which will help you determine whether or not a coat of arms for your family name exists. You may wish to research your family coat of arms or design one in the medieval tradition.

VERITAS LIBERAT

41

The Tournament

Imagine if you can a green field on a crystal clear spring day. High on a hill in the distance a white castle rises against the blue sky. In the center of the field, bright sunlight is bouncing off the shields of a hundred knights gathered on this day for the tournament.

Nearby in the galleries noblewomen sitting on wooden benches are busy exchanging castle gossip. They have much to say to each other as they have waited long and anxiously through the winter for this occasion. A soft breeze begins to blow from the south, and the veils attached to their cone-shaped hats billow in the wind.

On the edges of the field hundreds of townspeople and peasants mill around the grounds. The atmosphere is like that of a carnival. Jugglers, minstrels and dancers entertain and move among the crowd.

Suddenly the blare of a trumpet brings silence. Attention is drawn to the armored knights being lowered into their saddles. A herald shouts their names and recounts their many deeds of valor. The knights face each other at opposite ends of the wooden alleys. Attached to the helmet of one knight a lady's glove dangles. From the top of the other knight's helmet a veil unfolds in the breeze.

Once more the trumpet sounds. Both knights dig their spurs into the horses' sides and the charge begins. The horses race toward each other shaking the earth beneath their hooves. Above the cheers of the crowd, again and again the crack of lance upon lance and the thunder of lance upon shield is heard. The sounds are repeated until one knight is unseated. He falls helplessly to the ground. The winning knight dismounts and draws his sword. He stands above his foe and puts sword to throat. The fallen knight struggles to his knees, a sign of surrender. In this tournament the victor does not kill his opponent. Rightfully he can take his weapons, horse and armor or ask for a ransom. He chooses not to; instead he asks only that they exchange horses to mark this day.

The tournament will last several days. For experienced knights it is a time of renewed challenge; for others it is a time of receiving knighthood. For the young squires it may be their first mock battle. For in the Middle Ages tournaments were the training grounds for knights. At that time it was often said that a knight was not ready to do battle unless he was well-prepared even if it meant shedding his blood, cracking his teeth or breaking his bones.

The following terms were used in the description of a tournament. Can you define them?

valor	veil	lance	unseated
spurs	victor	mock	ransom

The Parts of a Castle

Use the descriptions below to identify the parts of a castle on page 44. Write the numbers of the parts described in the circles on the drawing.

1. The *outer bailey* was the first courtyard inside the outer walls of the castle.
2. The *inner bailey* was the inner courtyard of a castle. It was protected by two walls.
3. The *wall,* or *curtain* as it was sometimes called, surrounded the courtyard of the castle. Strongly built, it was not uncommon for the castle's walls to be ten or more feet in thickness.
4. The *keep* was known in French as the donjon. It was the strongest and most heavily fortified part of the castle as it was designed to be the last line of defense. Keeps were sometimes built round, sometimes square. Square keeps made nicer rooms, but round keeps were easier to defend. The keep usually housed the owner of the castle and his family. In it the great hall was often located. The great hall was the heart of the castle. It was used for family dinners, banquets, games, dancing, entertainment and sometimes a courtroom.
5. The *drawbridge* was a bridge which could be raised or lowered. It was usually located over a moat.
6. *Parapets* were low walls around the top edge of a tower or castle wall.
7. *Corbels* were stone projections in the walls which acted like brackets to support parapets.
8. *Machicolations* were the reason parapets were built. They were holes in the parapets used for dropping all kinds of things, such as boiling oil, hot water, stones, etc.
9. The *moat* was the ditch around the castle. It was usually filled with water.
10. The *barbican* was a foreward gate of the castle located before the main gate. It offered extra protection since the weakest part of the castle was considered to be the gate.
11. The *postern gate* was a back gate. It was supposed to be a secret, but oftentimes was not. The gate was used for attacking and surrounding the enemy outside the castle, as an escape, or for the coming and going of scouts and spies.
12. *Arrow-loops* were narrow openings in the castle's towers through which archers fired their arrows on the enemy below.
13. The *portcullis* was the main gate to the castle. It was made of very heavy wood and was reinforced with iron grating. Like the barbican, it could be raised or lowered for the protection of the people inside.
14. The *gatehouse* was the living quarters over the main gate of the castle. As time went on it became heavily fortified and very important. Sometimes the owner of the castle chose to live in the gatehouse.
15. *Murder holes* were holes in the ceiling just after the front gate. The holes were used for dropping large stones on attackers who got through the front gate.
16. *Rocky ledges* were important for the placement of castles. Castles built on rock could not be seized by tunneling.

The Parts of a Castle

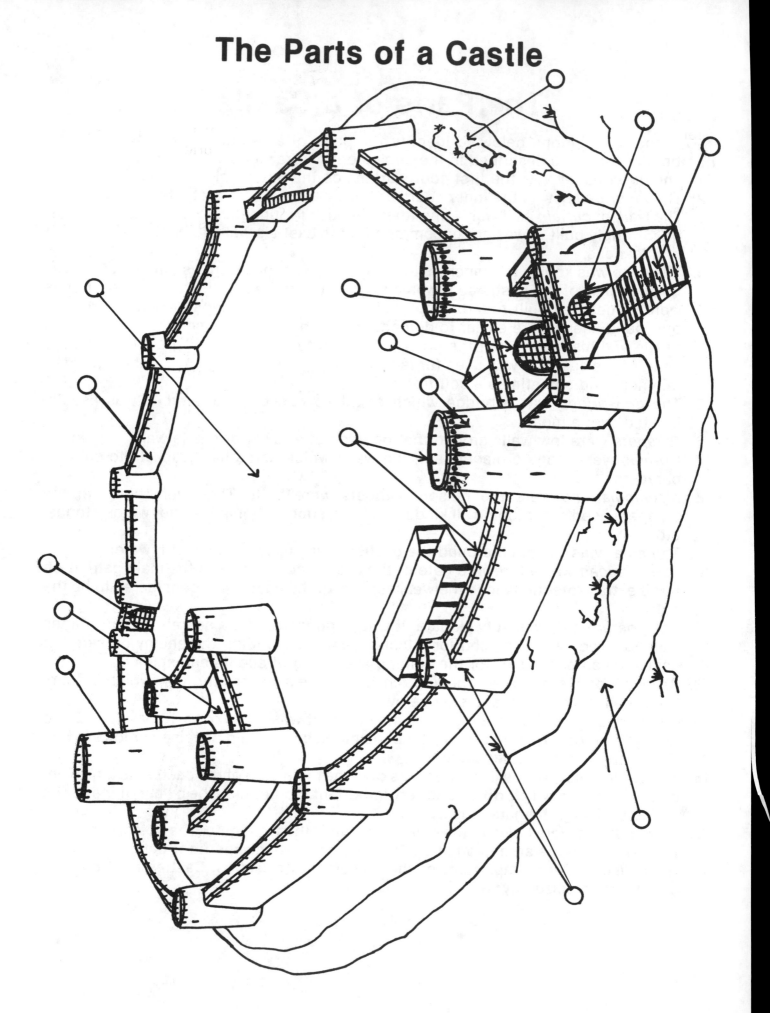

Offense or Defense?

Castles were more than homes for lords; they were fortifications against attack from their enemies. Even though castles were built to withstand heavy sieges, a great many castles were won and lost in battles several times over the centuries.

The surest way of taking a castle was by waiting. If the attackers had a lot of time, they waited until the people inside starved or surrendered; therefore, the most important defense of the castle was the ability to wait out the attack. This was usually done provided there was ample food and water in storage.

In protecting the castle as often as possible, the use of natural fortifications was taken into consideration. Castles built on high ground, rocky ledges, or the bend of a river were difficult to siege. Natural fortifications were not always possible, however, making the defense of the castle more difficult. As time went on, castle builders became very good at devising ways which would afford them every advantage in case of attack. Double and sometimes triple gates, stairways that spiraled to the right, and round towers instead of square all helped in the defense of the castle. As the castles became more difficult to capture, the weapons became more treacherous. Most of the weapons used in the Middle Ages were first used by the Romans with improvements as time went on. These devices used in ancient warfare are referred to by historians as engines of war.

On the following page are descriptions of devices and methods used in attacking (offense) and defending castles. Match the descriptions to the drawings on pages 47 and 48 and circle the word *offense* or *defense* (page 46) to tell whether the device or method was used in protecting or attacking a castle.

Use the italicized words in the descriptions to label the drawings.

Offense or Defense?

1. *Moat.* A ditch, usually filled with water, surrounding a castle. A *drawbridge* over the moat could be raised to prevent access to the castle. Offense or Defense

2. *Tunnel.* Perhaps the surest way of weakening a castle's wall. The tunnel was dug by men called sappers. The sappers propped the tunnel with timbers as they burrowed. When they reached the foundation, they removed stones until the wall was weak enough to collapse. Sometimes they set fire to the timbers causing the tunnel and the castle wall to collapse. Offense or Defense

3. *Ballista.* A gigantic crossbow which required several men to operate. The ballista was very powerful and accurate. The word *ballista* came from the Greek word *ballein* meaning to throw. Ballistics is a modern term taken from the same word. Offense or Defense

4. *Tower.* The tower was a roofed stairway on wheels. It was used to scale the high walls of a castle. It was usually covered with wet hides to prevent being set on fire. Towers could not be used where there was a moat, unless of course the moat was first filled in, which was sometimes done. Offense or Defense

5. *Machicolations or Holes.* Overhanging parts of the castle walls called parapets contained holes. When the castle was under siege, from these holes stones were dropped, boiling oil and water poured, or red hot iron thrown on the men below. Offense or Defense

6. *Battering Ram.* Widely used by the Romans, the battering ram continued to be popular well into the Middle Ages. It consisted of the largest and strongest tree trunk that could be found. The tree trunk was suspended on chains and housed in a shed with a roof and wheels. Sometimes the tip of the trunk was covered with metal spikes. As many as fifty men would swing the huge tree back and forth in its cradle against the castle wall. This usually went on nonstop until the wall was weakened and collapsed. Offense or Defense

7. *Portcullis.* A device for protecting the entrance to the castle. The portcullis was a gate usually made of heavy wood and iron crossbars. It was pulled up and down by chains and slid in specially carved grooves. Offense or Defense

8. *Trebuchet.* This device operated like a giant seesaw. The short end was heavily weighted down with stones. Many men were required to pull down the long end which when released fired a variety of unpleasant things such as huge stones or Greek fire, a burning mixture of chemicals, pitch and sulfur. Sometimes dead animals such as horses were shot over the castle's wall. The trebuchet was powerful and accurate. Offense or Defense

9. *Mangonel.* Usually shot heavy stones from a sling-like contraption. It was not as accurate but worked on the same principle as the *ballista.* Offense or Defense

10. *Postern gate.* A secret back gate to the castle. Its purpose was to allow the defenders to sneak out and surround their attackers. Offense or Defense.

11. *Rocky ledge.* Castles built on rock could not be threatened by tunnels. Ridges also gave the castle the advantage of height. Offense or Defense

12. *Thick walls.* It was not unusual for a castle to have walls ten or more feet thick. Offense or Defense

13. *Murder holes.* Holes in the flooring over the entrance just past the castle's front gate. If the attackers got through the gate, they were assaulted by heavy objects dropped through the holes from the ceiling above them. Offense or Defense.

14. *Arrow-loops.* Narrow openings in the towers of the castle just large enough for archers to fire their arrows on the enemy. Offense or Defense

Offense or Defense?

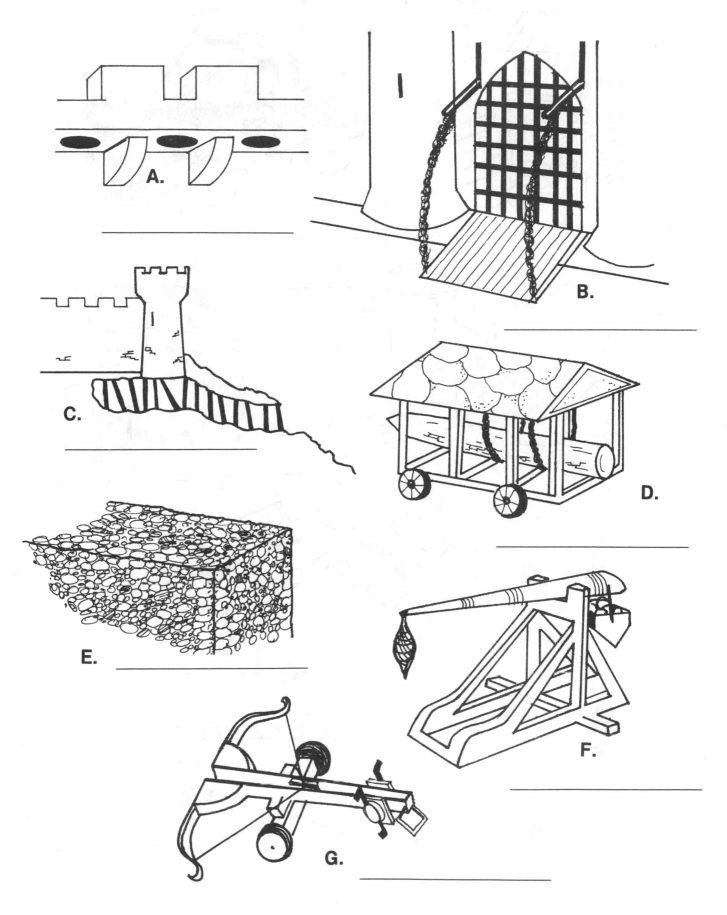

A. _____

B. _____

C. _____

D. _____

E. _____

F. _____

G. _____

Offense or Defense?

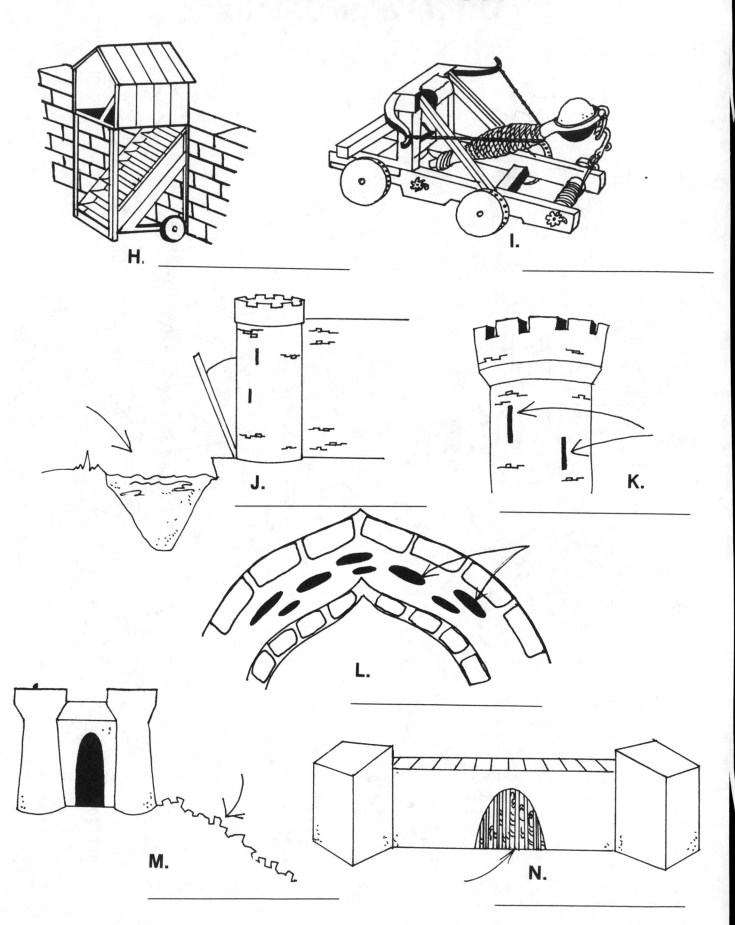

H. _____

I. _____

J. _____

K. _____

L. _____

M. _____

N. _____

48

Building Castles in the Air

1. Castles came in many shapes and sizes with no two exactly the same. Design a castle to suit your taste and style. Label its parts.
2. Why were castles important in the Middle Ages?
3. Research how castles changed from the early Middle Ages to late Middle Ages.
4. Why were many castles built near bodies of water, on the bends of rivers or on cliffs?
5. As time went on castles were replaced by palaces. What is the main difference between a castle and a palace?
6. The keep of a castle was once called a donjon in French. What modern word associated with castles comes from the word *donjon?*
7. In time, small villages and towns grew up around the castles. Why did people like to live near castles?
8. Discuss living in a castle. Would you like to have lived in a castle?
9. What conditions made castles cold, dark and damp?
10. What advantages does a small modern house have over a medieval castle?

Imaginary Animals

Imaginary animals were often used in heraldric shields and family crests. They are also the subject of many stories and tales which originated in the Middle Ages. Some of these imaginary creatures are popular in limited regions of only one country; others are known worldwide. The descriptions below are of imaginary animals not derived from mythology, but from folklore. Match the descriptions to the drawings on the next page.

1. The *griffin* or griffon has the head, wings and talons of an eagle, but its ears are similar to those of a dog. The lower half of its body is that of a lion. Griffons are guardians of gold and precious jewels. Their enemy is the horse. They are known throughout Europe.

2. The father of a *hippogriff* is said to be a griffin and its mother a horse. The hippogriff is a contradiction as horses and griffins are supposed to hate each other. The front half of a hippogriff resembles its father, a griffin; the rear resembles its mother, a mare. Hippogriffs are gentle creatures who love to graze. They are known throughout Europe.

3. The *unicorn* has the body of a horse, hind feet of a stag, the tail of a lion and a single horn on its forehead. It is known throughout the world as a symbol of purity.

4. The *senmurv* is part bird, part dog. Its head and forefeet are those of a dog, but it has the wings and tail of a bird. It is said to live in magic trees. Senmurvs are friendly creatures who cure evil. They are best known in Russia.

5. The *dragon* is known throughout the world. It is said to breathe fire. Its body is snakelike, but it has legs and sometimes wings. In early Christian times dragons symbolized evil, but to the Chinese they are honored symbols.

6. The *basilisk* is a small serpent with rooster-like head and wings. It is said to be able to destroy all life with a single look or its breath. It is known throughout Europe.

Imaginary Animals

Use the descriptions on the preceding page to make your own intrepretive drawings of these imaginary animals.

A _____

B _____

C _____

D _____

E _____

F _____

You Had to Be Smart to Play a Fool

Jesters were professional "fools" or jokesters whose job it was to amuse kings, nobles, and their families. Originally they were troubadours who sang and told gestes or stories of heroic deeds. As time went on jesters became buffoons or tellers of jokes. They began to be identified with a special type of suit made of half one color and the opposite half of another color. On their caps they sewed bells. They also wore long pointed shoes. Some jesters went to extremes to attract attention by shaving one half of their heads and half of the opposite side of their beards.

In some households the royal jesters became almost part of the family, and no doubt many of them were influential enough to give advice to kings.

In Shakespeare's play, *Hamlet,* he immortalized a court jester in a scene where the skull of Yorick, court jester to Hamlet's father, is dug up by gravediggers. Hamlet refers to Yorick as "a fellow of infinite jest, of most excellent fancy."

Questions:

1. What did jesters originally do? _____

_____

2. Why do you think jesters wore unusual clothing? _____

_____

3. Why were some jesters more important than just "fools"? _____

_____

4. What was the name of the jester immortalized in Shakespeare's play, *Hamlet?* ____

_____

5. Do you think Hamlet was fond of his father's jester? Why or why not? _____

_____

6. Who would be considered the jesters of today? _____

_____

7. What modern jesters wear costumes similar to medieval jesters? _____

_____

8. How has the audience of the "tellers of jokes" changed since medieval times? ____

_____

To make a jester of your own follow the directions on the next page.

Make a Court Jester

Trace the above pattern onto a piece of heavy paper or thin plywood. Cut the pieces out with scissors or a jigsaw.

Make a Court Jester

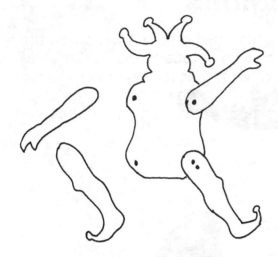

We are not "jest" kidding. Here are some ideas for using your jester.

Fasten the pieces together with round paper fasteners or small screws if you use wood.

Design a clown, pirate or animal and make a figure similar to that of the court jester.

Write dialogue for your jester. It can be amusing or advice from the jester to a king.

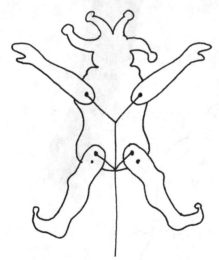

Make a jester or figure of your choice out of wood and present it as a gift.

Decorate a holiday tree with jesters adorned with glitter and sequins.

Attach string as shown.

Have a contest for the best-made jester.

Have a contest for the best jester joke.

Design a bulletin board for your teacher with jesters as the main attraction.

Your court jester will look like this when you are finished.

Three Great Religions

Christianity, Judaism and Islam are three religions which had great influence on the people and events in the Middle Ages as they continue to do in today's world. Some of the statements below are common to all three faiths; others refer to only one of these religions. Draw a small symbol of the faith in the blank to show which religion or religions match the statement. Remember, you can use more than one symbol when appropriate.

Star of David
Symbol of Judaism

Cross
Symbol of Christianity

Crescent and Star
Symbol of Islam

1._____ The followers believe in God.

2._____ Moses accepted the ten Commandments for this religion.

3._____ This religion calls God, Allah.

4._____ Their great religious teacher is Mohammed.

5._____ Their book of religious teaching is the Bible.

6._____ The early followers of this religion were called Disciples.

7._____ Their teachings are found in a book called the Koran.

8._____ Their teachings ask the followers to help the poor and the needy.

9._____ The followers are asked to pray five times a day facing Mecca.

10._____ The followers believe in the teaching of Jesus.

11._____ Their religious teachings and traditions are found in a book called the Talmud.

12._____ The people who accept this faith are called Muslims.

13._____ Their places of worship are called synagogues.

14._____ Their places of worship are called churches.

15._____ Their places of worship are called mosques.

16._____ Their book of wisdom and law is the Torah.

Medieval Tools

Medieval workers used many of the same tools we use today. They were usually made of wood and iron. Tools were expensive and not easily replaced. You can be certain that tools in this age were prized possessions and that the workers who used tools took good care of them. Can you match the drawings of the medieval tools on the next page to their names and functions below?

1._____ a measuring cord used like a tape measure
2._____ a square for testing right angles, straight lines, or plane surfaces
3._____ a small axe for chopping wood
4._____ a one-man saw for cutting wood
5._____ a two-man saw for cutting wood or stone
6._____ a level, a tool which shows if an object has an even horizontal surface
7._____ a trowel, a tool for putting mortar between stones
8._____ blacksmith's tongs, used for holding hot metal objects
9._____ a stonecutter's chisel used for splitting stone
10._____ a shovel for digging
11._____ a hoe for cultivating around plants or for mixing mortar
12._____ a crowbar used for prying or as a lever
13._____ a pickaxe used for breaking up stone or rock
14._____ a wedge used for splitting wood
15._____ a hammer for pounding nails or objects

Discussion Questions:

1. Which of the medieval tools pictured do we still use in basically the same form? __
   _____
   _____

2. Describe a modern level. _____
   _____

3. What advantages does a tape measure have over a measuring cord? _____
   _____

4. Describe a tool in three sentences. Read the description to your class. See how many of your classmates can name the tool you are describing. _____
   _____
   _____

Medieval Tools

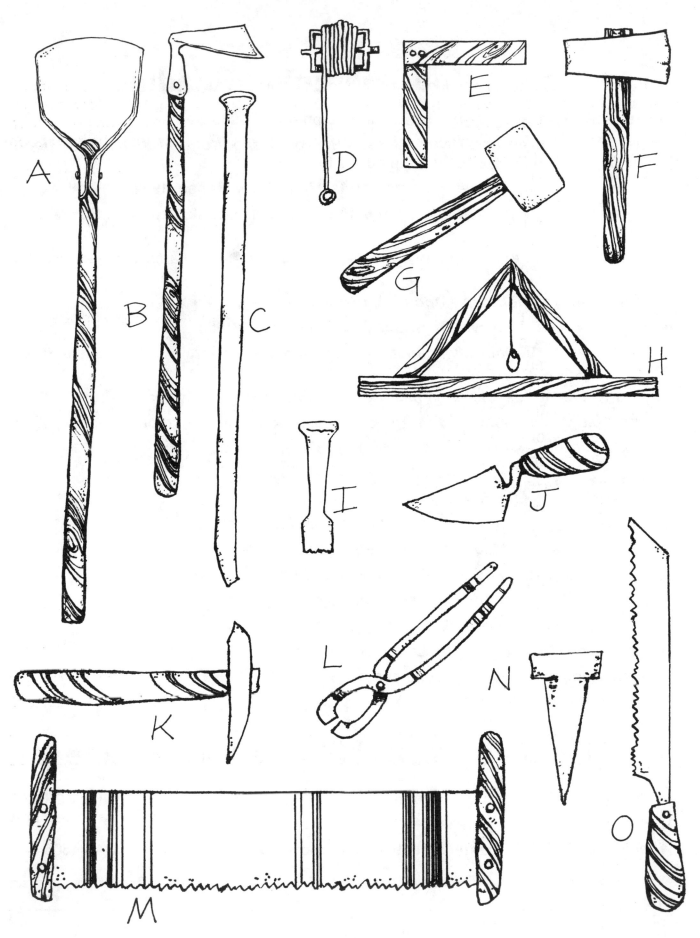

Books You Will Enjoy Reading

Brooks, Polly Schoyer. *Queen Eleanor.* J. P. Lippincott, 1983.

Brooks, Polly Schoyer and Nancy Zinsser Walworth. *The World of Walls: The Middle Ages in Western Europe.* J. P. Lippincott, 1966.

De Paola, Tomi. *Francis, The Poor Man of Assisi.* Holiday House, 1982.

Dugan, Alfred. *Growing Up in the Thirteenth Century.* New York. Pantheon Books, Inc., 1962.

Fremantle, Ann, and the Editors of Time-Life Books, *The Age of Faith.* Time-Life Books, 1965.

Glubock, Shirley. *Knights in Armour.* Harper & Row, 1969.

Hartman, Gertrude. *Medieval Days and Ways.* Macmillan, 1965.

Holmes, Urban T., Jr. *Daily Living in the Twelfth Century.* University of Wisconsin Press, 1952.

Kelly, Amy. *Eleanor of Aquitaine and the Four Kings.* Harvard University Press, 1950.

National Geographic Society, *The Age of Chivalry,* National Geographic Society, 1969.

Macaulay, David. *Castles.* Houghton Mifflin, 1977.

_____. *Cathedral.* Houghton Mifflin, 1973.

Mills, Dorothy. *The Middle Ages.* G. P. Putnam, N.D.

Paine, Albert Bigelow. *The Girl in the White Armour.* Macmillan, 1967.

Reeves, Marjorie. *The Medieval Monastery.* Longman, 1985.

_____. *The Medieval Town.* Longman, 1984.

Reeves, M. E. *The Norman Conquest.* Longman, 1984.

_____. *The Medieval Village.* Longman, 1984.

Turner, Derek. *The Black Death.* Longman, 1983.

Williams, Ann. *The Crusades.* Longman, 1973.

Filmstrips You Will Enjoy Watching

Medieval Knights. McIntyre Productions, Inc., 3238 Gillham Rd., Kansas City, MO 64109

Merry Ever After. Viking Press, 625 Madison Avenue, New York, NY 10022

When People Lived in Castles. Multi-Media Productions, Inc., Stanford, CA 94305

Answer Key

"WHAT SAY YE?" — Page 1

1. c
2. i
3. d
4. a
5. e
6. b
7. k
8. f
9. g
10. l
11. j
12. h

MODERN EUROPE — Page 4

1. Most of France, Italy, East and West Germany, Switzerland, Austria, Belgium and the Netherlands.
2. Charles.
3. Lothair
4. Louis
5. No.
6. No.
7. Answers will vary.
8. Answers will vary.

PEOPLE OF THE MIDDLE AGES — Page 7

A. Nun
B. Troubadour
C. Shepard
D. Pilgrim
E. Noblewoman
F. Knight
G. Monk
H. Serf
I. Bishop

LORD RANDAL — Page 8

1. Yes. He is a lord and has gold, silver, land, a house and cows.
2. No. 3. He was poisoned.
4. his true-love.
5. Definitely in the sixth stanza, but she probably suspected it earlier in the ballad.
6. Answers will vary.
7. His will.
8. Hell and fire.
9. Answers will vary.
10. Answers will vary.
11. Answers will vary.

MIND YOUR MANORS — Page 11

1. C
2. E
3. G
4. A
5. I
6. H
7. D
8. J
9. F
10. B

KNIGHTHOOD — Page 12

1. Good manners, courteous
2. Answers will vary.
3. Answers will vary.

KNIGHTHOOD — Page 13

1. squire
2. squire
3. page
4. squire
5. knight
6. page
Logical order: 3, 6, 1, 2, 4, 5

ARMOR — Page 15

1. A
2. K
3. M
4. I
5. J
6. C
7. D
8. G
9. L
10. B
11. H
12. F
13. N
14. E

WEAPONRY OF THE MIDDLE AGES — Page 17

1. J
2. H
3. B
4. D
5. E
6. A
7. G
8. F
9. I
10. C
11. K
12. L

DECORATIONS AND AWARDS — Page 20

Congressional Medal of Honor. USA. Given for risking one's life in an act of outstanding bravery. Military.

Order of the Purple Heart. USA. Wounded in action against the enemy. Military.

Iron Cross. Germany. Acts of bravery. Military.

Presidential Medal of Freedom. USA. Awarded to those who make significant contributions to American life. Civilian.

Croix de Guerre (pronounced kwaw duh gair). France. Awarded for acts of bravery. Military.

Victoria Cross. Great Britain. Awarded for outstanding bravery. Military.

Legion of Honor. France. Awarded for outstanding service to France. Military and civilian.

A THIRTEENTH CENTURY NOBLEWOMAN'S COSTUME — Page 22

A. coif
B. crespine
C. barbette
D. gown
E. cyclas
F. mantle
G. stocking
H. shoe

A FAMOUS LEGEND — Page 24

1. Lady Godiva
2. Someone who secretly looks at or watches other people.
3. Answers will vary.
4. Robin Hood, Johnny Appleseed, Paul Bunyan, etc.
5. Living person expected to be long remembered in stories, tales, etc.
6. Answers will vary.
7. Answers will vary.

A ROYAL FAMILY TREE — Page 28

1. Matilda
2. Henry I
3. No
4. Matilda; Geoffrey
5. From his father, Geoffrey
6. Five
7. They died before their father.
8. Richard
9. Geoffrey was already dead; John.
10. Henry II had already promised most of his kingdom to his other sons; he "lacked land" to give to John. John lived to become king.
11. A document which gave the people certain rights and privileges which John did not want them to have.
12. Two. Richard and John.

1 + 1 = WHO? Page 34
Top block to bottom.
King John II
William the Conqueror
Richard the Lion-Hearted
Lady Godiva
Charlemagne
Geoffrey
King Harold
Saladin
Eleanor of Aquitaine
Edward III

DECORATING THE SHIELD Page 38
Left to right: rampant, statant, couchant, passant.

A ROYAL COAT OF ARMS Page 40
1. C
2. F
3. A
4. D
5. G
6. B
7. E

THE TOURNAMENT Page 42
Valor—strength of mind or spirit that enables a man to encounter danger with firmness.
Veil—cloth worn by women as a covering for the head.
Lance—a weapon with a long shaft and a sharp steel head carried by mounted knights.
Unseated—to be knocked off one's horse.
Spurs—pointed devices on a rider's heel used to urge on a horse.
Victor—one that defeats an enemy or opponent.
Mock—an imitation.
Ransom—a consideration paid or demanded for release of a captured person.

THE PARTS OF A CASTLE Page 44

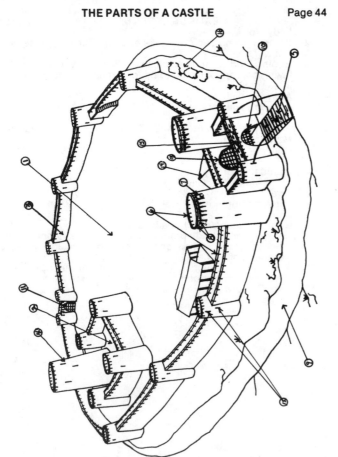

OFFENSE OR DEFENSE? Pages 47-48
A. Machicolations, defense
B. Portcullis, defense
C. Tunnel, offense
D. Battering ram, offense
E. Thick walls, defense
F. Trebuchet, offense
G. Ballista, offense
H. Tower, offense
I. Mangonel, offense
J. Moat with drawbridge, defense
K. Arrow-loops, defense
L. Murder holes, defense
M. Rocky ledge, defense
N. Postern gate, defense

BUILDING CASTLES IN THE AIR Page 49
1. Drawings will vary.
2. They were important as homes, for protection and as seats of government.
3. Answers will vary.
4. Protection.
5. Palaces are mainly homes for the wealthy and for nobility. They are usually not fortified.
6. Dungeon—the place where prisoners were kept.
7. For protection.
8. Answers will vary.
9. No central heat, small openings for windows, little light from candles or torches.
10. Answers will vary.

IMAGINARY ANIMALS Page 51
A. senmurv
B. hippogriff
C. unicorn
D. dragon
E. griffin
F. basilisk

YOU HAD TO BE SMART TO PLAY A FOOL Page 52
1. Originally jesters were troubadours who sang and told stories.
2. To attract attention.
3. They became close to the family, served as advisors and friends.
4. Yorick
5. Answers will vary.
6. Answers will vary.
7. Answers will vary.
8. Answers will vary.

THREE GREAT RELIGIONS Page 55
1. All three
2. Judaism
3. Islam
4. Islam
5. Christianity
6. Christianity
7. Islam
8. All three
9. Islam
10. Christianity
11. Judaism
12. Islam
13. Judaism
14. Christianity
15. Islam
16. Judaism

MEDIEVAL TOOLS Page 56
1. D
2. E
3. F
4. O
5. M
6. H
7. J
8. L
9. I
10. A
11. B
12. C
13. K
14. N
15. G